HAMMAD HASSAN

Travel Guide To Istanbul On A Budget In 2022 & Beyond

Discover The Top Attractions, Sights & Activities and Local Tastes To Explore In Istanbul, Türkiye For An Unforgettable Trip!

This book was professionally typeset on Reedsy.
Find out more at reedsy.com

*I dedicate this book to my amazing family
who supported me in the time of need.*

Travel! Your money will return. Your time won't.

Unknown.

Contents

1

Introduction

Merhaba fellow travelers! welcome to the travel guide to Istanbul, Türkiye on a budget in 2022 and for coming years. My name is Hammad Hassan and I feel very excited to be writing this guide book about Istanbul, one of my most favorite cities! You'll ask why Istanbul? Well, Traveling to Istanbul and other parts of Türkiye is safe, adventurous, thrilling and economical. Turkey renamed to Türkiye in 2022, is one of the World's most visited countries in 2019 with over 51 million visitors and it has a lot to offer! The landscape of Türkiye is very diverse ranging from beaches to mountains and to modern urban cities like Istanbul, a city where two continents collide. Spanning on both sides of the bosphorus, it is both physically and culturally part of Europe and Asia. Traveling to Türkiye has given me so much happiness and joy, and when I see others planning their own trip to Istanbul, I want them to love it as much as me by planning and preparing well to make the most out of their trip. Here is my attempt to do that.

A brief background about myself and how I feel about traveling.. Traveling is one of the most joyful experiences of life when done right. One who loves to travel, will try to capture every opportunity when possible. Travel takes us out of our comfort zone and inspires us to see, taste and try new things. It is the key to challenge yourself to adapt and explore new places, to engage with people that are different from us, to experience new adventures, learn a new language, taste something new, and most of all be brave enough to deal with all sort of situations, and to see how you'll deal with them on your own, improve your decision making skills on-spot and be surprise to see what you are capable of. It really brings us out of our nutshell! When I go through my decades old family albums, I see my mother holding me in her arms while traveling when I was two years old. That was my first trip!. In the coming years, I traveled through deserts at night and never knew how cold it gets even on a hot summer day or felt nauseated when traveling through mountains. All these new experiences at the time were unknown or few of them were disliked but what I didn't know was how much it'll instill in me and would make me want to travel when I grow up.

Fast forward to my graduation, I took a trip to Cuba with my friends and it was a mind blowing experience! As I began my career in the Fashion industry, I traveled a lot for work and took every opportunity to explore new places including Far East Asia, Middle East and Europe. I am glad I did! I was fortunate to travel to some parts of the world, making extra efforts to bend the rules, add a few days wherever possible in my professional or personal traveling and I still do it until today!

This book is not one that will give you every little detail about Istanbul, however i am writing this guide with the intention of providing 'to the point information' on-the-go that will help you maximize your time and have an unforgettable trip, without needing to flip through hundreds of pages to find what you are really looking for. For example, if you are at early stages of planning your trip, you can jump to the 'pre-planning, packing and travel documents' chapter, or if you are already in Istanbul and want to go sightseeing, you can read on the chapter of my most recommended attractions and activities in 'sights and activities' chapter. You want to explore cool neighborhoods or try a new dish, read through 'where to stay' or 'best dishes, desserts and drinks' chapter. This guide is simply here to provide the most condensed version and that's how I'd like a travel guide to be. And most of all, I hope you enjoy the chapters with tons of pictures to get a feel of the place or the food. With all those things said, let's jump right in!

2

Pre-planning, Travel Documents, and What To Pack

irst thing first, if you are planning your trip to Türkiye, step one is to book your flights in advance. But before you book, you need to know some basics! What season do you plan to visit? Keep in mind, if you are starting your trip from Istanbul, the best time to visit Istanbul is March to May and September to November. That's when most visited attractions are less crowded, room rates are affordable and daytime temperatures are between 60s and 70s Fahrenheit.

Booking Flights

It's always better to book your flights three to four months in advance if possible or at least six to eight weeks prior to your departure date. Avoid booking your flights in peak season from June to August, that'll cost you a higher fare and a higher accommodation cost. The tourism low season is November through March, if you can handle slightly colder weather. To get the best air fares, I always use skyscanner.com. They show you all the flights available from different airlines where you can choose the dates based on the best available airfare shown.

Budget tip- As far as the days of the week goes, check for deals on Mondays. You may also find cheapest flights on Tuesday morning depending on your location and avoid booking flights on Thursdays and over the weekend. Also, booking your flights through a connecting city will give you better airfare. And if you are lucky with your passport, you can also visit the connecting city on your way like I did when I was traveling to Türkiye through Switzerland.

Book your international and domestic flights if you have a confirmed itinerary. If you are traveling to Türkiye with multiple destinations like (Antalya and Cappadocia which are highly recommended), book your local flights on Turkish Airlines as the local flights are very reasonable (around $50-$70) and you can save more if you book three to four weeks in advance. Make sure to check your luggage allowance when booking because the price varies according to the luggage allowance.

Travel Documents, Travel Insurance and E-Visa

Make sure your passport has the minimum of six month validity and you'll most likely get an E-Visa from https://www.evisa.gov.tr/en/ even if you have an American or Canadian passport. Post-pandemic traveling situations have brought new regulations, check your country's travel rules for the destination you are traveling to and make sure you are prepared. Most likely, you'll also need the health declaration form for entry to Türkiye prior to your travel. You can visit https://register.health.gov.tr/ and fill in your details! This form will also help you to activate your Istanbul metro card called 'Istanbulkart', a must have when staying for a few days in Istanbul. It's always better to get travel insurance as you never know what circumstances you may go through while traveling.

The cost of travel insurance ranges from $50 to $200 for a two week trip depending on your location and selection of the type of insurance.

Don't forget to check if your credit card comes with built-in travel insurance. If you have gold or platinum credit cards, they often offer free travel insurance. Check with your credit card provider for details. Once you have your passport, e-visa and other travel documents all sorted out, it's time to get to packing!

What to pack and pack light (you'll shop till you drop)

A little bit about fashion as i have worked in the fashion and apparel industry on the design and buying side of the business. Türkiye has a strong textile/fashion industry with many local brands that focus on trendy clothing inspired from European fashion. They also export home and fashion apparel to major European fashion brands and have their own design house and factories that are well equipped and developed to compete with the international fashion industry. Having said that; Turkish millennials and Gen-z dress very well and if you are someone who likes to dress trendy while traveling, Istanbul is your spot! I love to shop for myself and for the family whenever I am traveling in Istanbul. The price points are great and you can find trendy fashion clothing on a low to medium price point.

The most common mistake when packing for traveling is your tendency to pack everything that you can and not knowing what to pack realistically for your destination. The best way of traveling is always light ! Istanbul is an amazing shopping destination. You'll find the best fashion, home decor and local souvenirs to buy. Yet, you better have the room to pack all that shopping and that would only be possible if you are packing light for traveling! Keeping the climate in mind depending on when you plan to travel, you'll need to be mindful of what to pack;

In Spring (Apr – May) and Autumn (Oct–Nov)

You may encounter rain, and the air may be cool or even chilly at night, but comfortable during the day, pack a sweater and a windbreaker in case.

In Summer (Jun – Sep)

Wear everyday summer clothing. You may bring a sun hat and a sunblock along with your wardrobe. Have a few light layers for cool evenings when needed. It gets chilly by the seaside!

In Winter (Dec – Mar)

You'll need warm clothing like hoodies, sweatshirts, knit sweaters and a warm jacket. It snows in December and January, you'll need the beanies and scarves to cover up for the cold!

Here's a short list of what to pack for your trip if you are traveling in the recommended season;

- Few pair of jeans, khakis and shorts for men
- T-shirts, button down and a sports blazer for men
- T-shirts, tops and blouses for women
- Long flowy dresses, long skirts and jeans for women
- Comfortable pair of running shoes and sandals – men and women
- Sweaters/layers for cold nights
- Rain jacket and umbrella for rainy days
- Sun hats, caps and sunblocks for the hot summer days
- Scarves and cover-ups for mosque entrances – women
- Turkish electrical adapter
- A good camera if you are a fan of photography (not to miss the sights)

- Packing cubes and pouches
- Travel insurance (a must!)
- Bathing suites or shorts for Hammams
- An extra phone, USB cables (recommended but not necessary)
- An extra luggage that you can buy from there for all the shopping that you don't want to miss!

3

Creating Itineraries and Budgeting

The best trip starts with a good planning! Researching about your destination and creating a **smart itinerary** will make a huge difference in your trip experience and I can not stress this enough! I strongly recommend researching your destination and creating an itinerary that includes budgeting and daily planning of what places you want to visit, activities, food, shopping and exploring to make the most out of your trip and be flexible!

You may use itinerary templates from canva.com or download a standard template from google. I use an app called **'visit a city'** which is free to use, where i select the destination, number of days and it produces the itinerary for me based on my preference. I use this app every time I am visiting a new city and I love it! It can give you a jam packed itinerary or an easy going depending on your traveling preferences. You can add in your hotel location and it'll even guide you through maps and links to buy tickets for top attractions if you haven't already! I have traveled Asia and Europe through this app and it has really made exploring the cities easy for me instead of spending hours and hours searching online!

Budgeting

Travel expenses and trip costs depend on your budget, affordability and how flexible you are with the finances. But as we are planning to travel on a budget, here goes my tips and recommendations to travel on a budget based on average daily expenses per person;

Flights

Flights are one of the significant parts of your trip cost. It totally depends on where you are flying from and what season did you book your travel in? You can also choose budget airlines like Ryanair, Easyjet, Pegasus or Vueling Airlines to reduce the airfare if you are traveling from Europe. Here are some average costs to expect:

- **Europe** (London, Barcelona, Amsterdam etc.) Very low fares ranging from $150 - $350
- **North America** (USA, Canada) High fares compared to Europe ranging from $800 - $1200
- **Asia** (South East Asia) Moderate fares compared to North America, ranging from $600 - $1000

(Source: skyscanner.com, based on 1.5 to 2 months in advance flights availability)

Accommodation

- Hostels. $25 - $40 (based on shared accommodation)
- Low-price hotels. (1-2 stars) Under $50
- Med-price hotels. (2-3 stars) $50 - $70
- Med-high price hotels. (3-5 stars) $80 - $150

Based on off-season average prices observed from Booking.com and my personal experience. Try to find an accommodation with breakfast included and no cancellation fee if your plan changes. Be flexible with your bookings.

Meals

Breakfast. Preferably included in your accommodation, if not grab a simit and a coffee for under $3. Lavish breakfast, a must experience while in Türkiye, add $10 to your daily budget.

- Lunch. $5 - $10 per meal
- Dinner. $5 - $10 per meal
- Dessert, coffee or ice cream. $2 - $5

Total= **$25** for all if you don't eat from expensive restaurants.

Transportation

I'd highly recommend getting an 'Istanbulkart' to travel on the Metro. Metro is the most convenient and cheapest way to travel to most of the attractions in Istanbul. You can use the same card to travel on trams and ferries to keep the travel cost low between $5 - $10 if traveled to multiple sites in a day, otherwise your traveling cost could be under $5 if you mix it up with metro and on-foot. Top up your istanbulkart when needed. I'd usually top up with 100 Lira and it'll last for a few days.

Sights and Activities

It depends on your wish list, the more you see the more you'll pay!

(depending on museums and other activities that require a big budget like Big Bus/cruise tours, Museums, water activities etc). An average daily expense of $25 to $50 is sufficient for daily activities.

Excluding the entertainment and sightseeing, you can live, eat, commute and enjoy many free sights under **$70 or more** per day if traveling on a budget.

4

Best Time To Travel

Weather is great In Istanbul through spring and autumn. The summers are warm, humid and sunny but pleasant at night and the winters are cold, windy, partly cloudy and occasionally snows through December to February. The best time to travel is between

Mar - May and Sep - Nov.

Istanbul is a big city and can keep you engaged for a couple of weeks if you like exploring! I recommend spending at least **4 - 7 days** to get a true taste of Istanbul. Anywhere less than four days, it won't do the justice to this magnificent city!

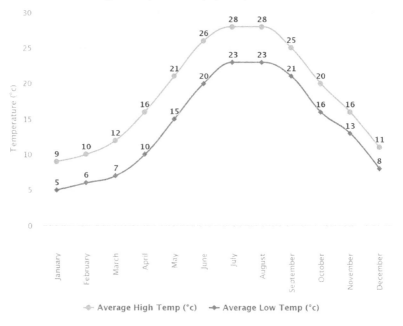

Source: worldweatheronline.com

5

Orientation To Istanbul

I stanbul is a magnificent melting point of history and cultures, the only city in the world to hold the geographical position of spanning on two continents, Europe and Asia. Formerly known as Constantinople and Ancient Byzantium, officially adopted the name in

1930 to Istanbul, is the largest city and principal seaport of Türkiye, serving as the country's economic, cultural and historic hub. Its population is over 15 million people, equal to 19% of the country's population. The city's geographical position and it's rich history, traditional and modern culture, variety of food, outstanding shopping and historical sights and activities attracts tourists from all over the world, making it one of the most visited cities globally. Istanbul is vibrant, fun and a lively city with more than eighty museums to visit, international film, music and theater festivals, art galleries showcasing cultural, arts, paintings, sculpture and photography.

The cafe culture is very popular in Istanbul, you'll see beautiful cafes in most touristic areas where people are just sitting and enjoying their evenings and free time. Çay and Kahve are an essential part of Turkish culture. The variety of desserts I came across in Istanbul was so tempting! If you are a foodie and have the sweet tooth like I do, you are in trouble! Another surprising sight was when I saw cats and dogs in shops, hotels and stores sitting around. People are very friendly and caring when it comes to Cats and dogs, in fact the City has an official 'Stray Dogs and Cats' program in which stray animals are protected by Turkish Law. Istanbul is also the beauty hub for hair transplants and personal care for men and women. You'll see a lot of men walking around with head bandages on the streets and women wearing bandages on their noses. Nevertheless, Istanbul will keep on surprising you wherever you go.

Separated in two parts by the Bosphorus strait, Istanbul's Bosphorus strait runs for about twenty miles that joins the Sea of Marmara with the Black Sea in Istanbul. Bosphorus strait is a natural waterway located in Northwestern Turkey. Istanbul is divided in three parts, *the Bosphorus Strait* which acts as a dividing line between Europe and asia. Then comes the *Golden horn* separating the western part and the Sea of Marmara. Most sights are located in the old city of *Sultanahmet*, to the west of Bosphorus, between the Horn and the Sea. The heart of modern Istanbul where most tourists roam around and spend their days is across the Horn to the north are *Galata, Beyoglu* and *Taksim* that are in Beyoglu district of the European side of the city.

6

Airports (Havalimani) and Transportation

Türkey accommodate over 45 million inbound visitors in 2019 and 24.7 million international tourists in 2021, a decline due to pandemic but it is getting back to full swing in 2022. The new Istanbul airport was opened in 2019 with 90 million passengers per annum capacity, making it the largest airport in Europe now. Istanbul airport also ranked second in the world Top 10 airports list. There are two airports connecting to the city;

Istanbul new airport (IST) which is on the European side of the city. Stay informed that Atatürk airport is closed to passenger flights. If traveling by a taxi to Istanbul new airport **(IST)**, your route should be on **D020** highway, or O-3 to turn north on O-7.

Connecting to the city is easy. You can take the Public Taxi from the airport to Taksim, Galata or Sultanahmet which'll cost around 300-350 Lira (one way) and about 45 minutes to an hour depending on traffic. You can also take **Havaist Buses** that are available at numbered gates on level -2 of the airport, departing periodically to different parts of the city. You can get Istanbulkart from one of the machines and top it up with cash in local currency only. This is the most affordable option to get to the city center as the bus route goes through regular lanes. It usually costs between 30-50 Lira and about 1 to 1.5 hours depending on the traffic. Keep in mind the fare cost is also variable with the exchange rate.

-**Sabiha Gökçen Airport** (SAW) is located 30km east of the city center. It is on the Asian/Anatolian side of the city. Many domestic and budget flights from Europe depart and arrive from SAW. The best way to commute economically from SAW to the city center is by Havaist or Havabüs. It'll cost between 30-50 Lira by cash and a long commuting time of 90 minutes or more.

Transportation

Istanbul has a good public transport system with Metro, Rail and Tram lines. There are six metro lines, the first has two branches. The most useful to most tourists is **M1A** and the **M2** which passes near Sultanahmet and travels to Galata/Taksim and beyond. There's an extensive bus system, including city run and private buses that commute with-in and inter-city with affordable fare accepted in cash in local currency, Turkish Lira (TRY). You can also find taxis everywhere but be careful with the taxi drivers as some of them will try to take longer routes to make some extra cash. Always ask to turn on the meter and check if the seal on the meter is intact. Try to take the metro and trams instead of taxis if you are traveling to see tourist sights as the local traffic is very congested and it'll cost you a lot of time and increased fare to commute by taxi. There are also local minivans called Dolmus that run all night long and can be easily found on Taksim square for local and intercity traveling, make sure to keep the cash in local currency to pay for the fare.

An easy way to get around in the city is to download city maps, use google maps that tells you the time and options of commuting to get to your destinations. You can also use other apps such as 'Trafi' If you plan to stay in Istanbul for a few days as it's recommended due to the city has so much to offer. Again, it is highly recommended to buy 'istanbulkart'. You can get the card at one of the vending machines at metro and rail stations. Keep in mind, the display will be in Turkish language but you can select the English or other languages to understand and choose your options. You should also top up the card at the same time to avoid lineups and an uninterrupted commuting for a good one week. The best thing about 'Istanbulkart' is that you can use it on most modes of transportation especially in metro, trams and ferries. There are also docks or piers in Karaköy, Eminönü and Sultanahmet where you can commute through boat cruises and ferries to get to the Asian side of the city. Karaköy and Eminönü docksides are a great option to take the ferry to get to Kadiköy and Möla which are great local neighborhoods to discover the Asian side of Istanbul.

Due to the pandemic, you'll need to link your HEC code with your Istanbulkart that you'll get by registering on https://register.health. gov.tr prior to your traveling. The linking of your HEC code will help you travel on metro and trams. You can link the code by going to the metro office located at metro stations where they'll check your health document in printed or digital form and verify the code. This was mandatory when I was traveling in late 2021 and early 2022 but it could be removed due to the ease of covid restrictions in recent months of Spring 2022.

7

Where To Stay, Best Budget Hostels

I stanbul has hundreds of hotels, airbnb and hostels all across the city. There are two main sides to pick and start your journey. Asian side and European side! Most tourists who visit Istanbul stay in Beyoglu district on the European side due to ease of commuting, top attractions, food, shopping and nightlife. There are six main districts/areas to choose depending on your travel expectations. Below are my most recommended areas to stay with an alert of staying vigilant and safe;

Sultanahmet (The Old Town)

The most visited area of Istanbul, Sultanahmet! It is the historic and cultural center of Istanbul where you can visit all the main attractions and sights all nearby accessible by tram, on-foot or by car. If you are visiting Istanbul for the first time, this is your place to stay, eat and explore.

Galata (Known for nightlife)

My personal favorite and another recommended area to stay for the true flavor of Istanbul. Galata is located north of the Golden Horn. Galata is a place where you can walk along the cobbled streets and enjoy the magnificent views of Galata Tower and the surrounding area full of restaurants, hotels, shops selling local souvenirs, fridge magnets, crockery, merchandise and home decor products. It is the part of Beyoglu district that connects with other parts like karakoy and taksim. The istiklal street goes all the way from Galata tower to Taksim Square. It's an enjoyable stroll in the day or late night always packed with locals and tourists eating, shopping, singing or just roaming around. Galata bridge is another great place to go for a walk or to watch a sunset with tons of locals hanging their fish rods over the bridge. You can go under the bridge to have a snack or dinner with stunning views of the Bosphorus river. Galata is perfect if you want to stay close to Karakoy, Taksim or

Sultanahmet. And most of all, you can party till morning as there are alot of bars and clubs in this area.

Karaköy (Best for young travelers with a budget)

Let me say it out loud, I stayed in Karaköy twice and I loved it! It is one of the coolest neighborhoods and my most favorite place to chill, dine and relax. You can find decent accommodations, restaurants with live music, cafes and bars and tons of cool crowds to mingle with. I stayed at Casa Rosa on my first visit and instantly made friends with the two gentlemen Omar and Taifur. They were both very helpful and easy to hang out with so we went to have a nice dinner where I tried 'Iskender kebab' a must-have dish when in Istanbul.

The best thing about staying in Karaköy is to step out of your hotel and just walk to the pedestrian street where you can find all the good restaurants, cafes, bars and boutique shops all located on the same street. And while you are at it, catch a place with live music if that comforts your soul! You can also walk about ten minutes to Karaköy pier to catch a commuter ferry and go to Kadiköy which is located on the Asian side of the city. Ther Ferry itself is an awesome experience especially if taken at the time of the sunset. You'll be welcomed by a bunch of seagulls and passengers getting to the other side of the city. Another advantage of staying in Karaköy is to take the T1 tram from Tophane station and visit Eminönü for shopping, Sirkeci for turkish delights, figs and dried apricots and Sultanahmet for the historic sights. By far this is my most recommended area to stay if you want to get away from the crowded Taksim square full of tourists and experience the local contemporary culture of Istanbul.

Grand Bazaar (For a family trip)

Grand Bazaar is one of the oldest shopping bazaars in the world. It is also a highly recommended place to visit and the main old shopping area of Istanbul. If you are visiting with family and want to stay close to the main attractions in Sultanahmet, love shopping with bargains, enjoy the traditional restaurants, street culture and various hotel options, this is your place to stay! Grand and Spize Bazaar are full of shopping opportunities and the area outside the Bazaars have tons of street vendors with shopping options. It is crowded during the daytime and calm at night so you can enjoy the day doing activities and relax at night.

Taksim (For First Timer and late-nighters)

One of the most popular and crowded areas in Istanbul is Taksim, which is located in Beyoglu district. It is convenient and a preferred choice to stay for a lot of tourists. The main attraction of this area is Taksim Square and Istiklal Street that is lively day and night! You'll find a wide range of hotels from luxury to mid-range to backpacker hostels along with restaurants, shopping and nightlife. The best part, you can take the metro and go to Cevahir mall, Istinye park mall for a shopping spree or head to Galata and the other parts of the city in no time. I stayed here twice and enjoyed the convenience but it was too touristy for me so I moved to Karaköy to enjoy the local culture of the city. If you want to stay away from the crowded touristic areas like Taksim, I would recommend staying in Karaköy. If you are traveling solo and want to save money, stay in hostels and make new friends to explore Istanbul together.

Kadiköy - The Asian side

Kadiköy, the center of the Asian side that shows the true colors of the local culture. It has beautiful views of Bosphorus and the old Istanbul, a great variety of local shopping markets, traditional restaurants and affordable living accomodations. As recommended earlier, if you are staying in Karaköy, hop on to a commuter ferry from Karaköy or Eminönü pier for under a dollar or two and enjoy the forty minutes of ferry ride looking at the beautiful architecture of Istanbul from the Golden Horn.

Once settled down, put on a pair of comfortable shoes and head to Moda caddesi to the Tea Gardens to enjoy the panoramic views of the Marmara sea and the old Istanbul. Visit the seaside promenade that begins at the Kadiköy ferry docks or head to 'Baghdad Avenue', the main commercial street offering upscale boutiques, cafes, restaurants and bars. People are friendly and ready to help or guide however they can. Be flexible, enjoy the local hospitality of the Asian side of the city and connect to the culture!

Best Budget Hostels

Although you are sharing the space with other people in hostels, the best thing about backpacking and staying in hostels is to meet new people, hangout together and make friends. The best part, you save tons of money and get to see the best of the city on a budget by taking the free Istanbul walking tours if you like to explore on-foot or go to a pub crawl to explore nightlife! All these hostels below are on a rating of **9 or above** on booking.com

- **Stay Inn Taksim**
- **Bauhaus Guesthouse**
- **Cheers Hostel**
- **Archeo**
- **Hostel Le Banc**

8

Sights and Activities

B yzantine meets Ottoman, Istanbul is one of the world's greatest cities with centuries old history and rich culture. The city mesmerizes you with its historical sights, Bosphorus river and beautiful sunsets behind the stunning architectures of the mosques with their colorful tile work. There's so much to explore in the city with sights, food, shopping and activities that i had to narrow it down well for you to make the most memorable trip! I haven't added the timings or entrance fee information for each attraction as it's better to book it online, in-advance or on the go for the sake accuracy.

Here are my top recommended sights and activities while your stay in Istanbul;

Istanbul Archaeological Museum & Museum of Turkish and Islamic Arts

The Archaeology Museums are a group of three museums: Archaeological Museum, Museum of the Ancient Orient and Museum of Islamic Art, located in the Eminönü square near Gülhane Park and Topkapi Palace.

Eminönü is the hotspot on the southern side of the Galata bridge on the European side.

The Turkish Islamic Art Museum is the first museum to offer Turkish and Islamic art together.It has the world's richest Islamic art collection. The museum offers an incredible opportunity to learn about islamic culture and history. It displays a variety of impressive islamic calligraphy, Turkish rugs, exquisite ceramics and wood carving.

Chora Church (Kariye Camii)

The Kariye Mosque, formerly known as the Chora Church was a Greek Orthodox church, is renowned worldwide for its well-preserved mosaics and frescoes. Tourists from all over the world love to visit this place for its beautiful mosaics work.

Gülhane Park

Gülhane Park (rose garden or the house of roses garden) is the oldest urban park in Istanbul, located in Eminönü and the neighborhood of Sultanahmet. It is also one of the most beautiful and largest parks of Istanbul. When visiting Hagia Sophia and Topkapi Palace, it is a must to add to your itinerary if you are a fan of parks and beautiful city views.

Dolmabahçe Palace

Dolmabahçe Palace was built in the 19th century during the Ottoman empire, located in Besiktas. The palace has impressive European and Ottoman style interiors, 285 rooms and 43 Halls. The formal garden displays stunning fountains and flower beds.

Topkapi Palace

Topkapi Sarayi or Topkapi Palace exhibits the imperial collection of the Ottoman Empire and maintains an extensive collection of books in the library. This enormous palace was the residence of Ottoman Sultans for almost 400 years. It has many exhibition halls, treasury section and Harem. Topkapi palace was not only the residence of Sultans but also the administrative and educational center of the state. It is located on the Sarayburnu (seraglio point), which overlooks both the Marmara sea and the Bosphorus Strait. The T1 tram is the most convenient way to get to the Sultanahmet area which only takes a five minute walk to Topkapi palace from the Sultanahmet station.

Spice Bazaar

Spice Bazaar, built in 1664, is one of the oldest and largest bazaars of Istanbul that offers a huge variety of colorful spices, Turkish delights, dried fruits and nuts, seeds, herbs and much more. One station down from Sultanahmet, it is a must-visit and should be planned together with Grand Bazaar. Both places get very crowded so try to come earlier in the day or after 4pm to dodge the crowds.

Grand Bazar (Kapali çarsi)

Istanbul's Grand Bazaar is one of the world's oldest bazaars built in 1461. It has over 4000 shops selling carpets, famous Turkish lamps, local souvenirs, ceramics, jewelry, bags and much more. Make sure to put on your bargain hat and make the best deal before buying.

Blue Mosque (Sultanahmet Camii)

The magnificent Sultan Ahmed Mosque (Sultanahmet Camii), also known as The Blue Mosque due to the blue tiles used inside the interiors and walls, was built between 1609 and 1616. It is one of the most beautiful mosques in the world. It is also one of the most popular attractions in Istanbul and attracts a large number of tourists from all over the world. Best way to see the great architecture of the mosque is to approach it from the west side of the mosque or from the Hippodrome. Mosque étiquettes include taking off your shoes and wearing full length/moderate clothing that covers your body is applicable to men and women both.

Taksim Square

Taksim Square is the heart of Beyoglu, located in the European side of Istanbul. The Square hosts major tourists coming for food, shopping, hotels and nightlife. There is an easy access to the metro station right in the square, from where you can travel to major destinations in the city including to Cevahir and Istinye park mall. The Square is connected to Istiklal street and stays busy most of the time where locals and tourists get together to enjoy food and drinks.

Istiklal Street

Istiklal Street (İstiklal Caddesi) is the most famous and busiest street in Istanbul. It is a 1.4km long pedestrian street that runs from Taksim Square to the famous Galata Tower. It is one of my most favorite and recommended long walks when in Istanbul. The street is packed with locals and tourists day and night and is famous for amazing food, cafes, famous fashion brand's shopping and local souvenirs. You'll come across a crowd of people gathered to sing and dance with a bunch of guys singing live just to enjoy and have fun.

Galata Tower

The Galata tower (Galata Kulesi) is one of the most prominent historical landmarks of Istanbul. It is a beautiful tower that is surrounded by restaurants, hotels and shops. You can walk from Taksim square to Galata Tower through Istiklal Street which is a highly recommended activity on your tour. Catch a beautiful sunset by getting up to the tower right before sunset and enjoy the city views.

The Magnificent Ayasofya / Hagia Sophia

Your trip will be incomplete if you don't visit this glorious and magnificent architectural marvel of Türkiye, Hagia Sophia (Ayasofya). It was chosen as a UNESCO world heritage site in 1985. Officially the Hagia Sophia Grand mosque now, it was once a church, later converted to a museum and now officially a grand mosque again in 2020.

Precaution: Be alert of pocket pickers with your purses, bags and belongings and never put them in your back or side pockets of your pants.

Top Activities not to miss!

- Bosphorus sunset cruise
- Hop on Hop off Big Bus city tours
- Make a day trip to Princess Island
- Visit Golden Horn, Eminönü, Sirkeci in Sultanahmet
- Watch whirling Dervishes at Galata Mevlevi
- Listen to live music with dinner in Karaköy
- Get a bath at Hammam
- Try catching an ice cream cone on istiklal street
- Take the commuter ferry from Eminönü to Kadiköy and enjoy the Asian side of Istanbul
- Admire the Art in Istanbul Modern – museum of modern art

9

Best Dishes, Desserts and Drinks

Turkish Breakfast

Unlike other countries, Turkish breakfast has a good variety of food made in different portions like bread, butter, various cheeses, boiled and fried eggs, sausages, olives, simit, figs, dried apricots and much more along with Turkish çay and coffee. Turkish breakfast leaves you content and full of energy for the rest of the day!

Most Delicious Turkish Food

Turkish cuisine is rich, flavorful and irresistible, making it one of the best cuisines in the world. Like the country's rich and diverse culture, Turkish cuisine is also very diverse, evolved from Mediterranean, Balkan, Middle eastern and Central asian cuisines. It has also fused over the time with European and international cuisines, bringing a range of modern fusion food to the menu. Here are my traditional must-try Turkish cuisine recommendations;

Dürüm

Dürüm is one the most popular street food that is delicious, filling and easy on the pocket. It is a wrap filled with layers of chicken or beef put on rotisserie, vegetables and sauces. The most common bread used for

45

the wrap is lavash. When the wrap is made, it is usually put on the flat grill to make it warm and add some grill marks for the presentation.

Döner Kebap

Döner Kebab is similar to Dürüm but in an open bread. The meat is sliced from rotisserie, put into a flat open bread topped with vegetable salad, sauces filled with chicken or beef and wrapped in a paper. It is also served on a platter with rice, sliced rotisserie chicken on beef, salad and fried.

Iskender Kebap

Iskender Kebap is one of the most popular dishes of Turkish cuisine. It has thin sliced layers of Döner kebab on top of bread with tomato sauce, grilled peppers and tomatoes on the side, served with yogurt.

Börek (baked filet pastries)

Börek is a savory Turkish pastry often served at breakfast and brunch. There are many shapes and sizes og Borek. It's a flaky dough filled with ingredients like cheese, spinach, potatoes, chicken or any other vegetables.

Pide

Pide or Turkish pizza is an oval shaped flatbread baked with various combinations of toppings like cheese, vegetables, chicken or beef depending on your choice.

Sis Tavük

Tavük sis is a traditional bbq Turkish dish where chicken is marinated with subtle spice and flavors. It is put on a skewer to grill to perfection over hot charcoal, served with flatbread, rice and salad.

Lahmacun

Lahmacun, literally means 'dough with meat', also known as Turkish thin pizza, is a famous street food all over Turkey. It is a thin layer of dough topped with minced meat and a variety of vegetables.

Kumpir (baked potato)

Kumpir is a Turkish style baked potato, cut open and filled with delicious toppings like butter, cheese, corn, vegetable salad, pickles, green and black olives and much more. Depending on your choice, you can keep it all veggie or add meat.

Köfte Ekmek

Another popular street food, Köfte Ekmek or meatball sandwich is stuffed with small meat patties cooked on a grill and served in a bread like a sandwich filled with tomatoes, onions, and salad.

Adana Kebab

Adana Kebabs are made of minced lamb or beef seasoned with cumin, sumac, red pepper flakes and a few other ingredients to enhance the flavor. It is one of the most popular kebabs in Turkish cuisine. Adana Kebabs are long, hand-minced kebabs that are cooked over a hot charcoal grill and served on a platter with thin bread rice, grilled tomatoes, peppers, onions and salad.

Continental Cuisine

My personal recommendation to try anything from continental menu. You'll love the modern Turkish cuisine and the classic burgers, steaks and pastas!

- **Grilled Cheese Burger** from Mezbaa, Baltazar or Root burger house in Karaköy.
- **Tavuk Dünyasi** is also recommended if you wanna try Thyme, Buffalo or Creamy mushroom chicken served with pasta and salad.
- My most favorite spot for food, coffee and dessert is **MADO** that you can find everywhere in Istanbul.

Street Food

If you are strolling on the streets of Istanbul and craving for quick bites, you can always grab one of the popular street foods and get a quick energy refill in your body to keep going.

- Roasted chestnuts
- Boiled and grilled corn
- Balik sandwich (fish)
- Simit
- Tantuni (beef wrap)
- Mussels or Midye Dolma

Turkish Coffee (kahve)

Turkish coffee (kahve) is strong, rich and delightful. It is brewed in a copper coffee pot called 'cezve' using ground coffee beans over the hot charcoal without filtering it. Kahve is a big part of Turkish culture that is enjoyed on the streets, cafes and restaurants all over Türkiye.

Turkish Çay

Turkish Çay is a cultural symbol and the sign of hospitality. It is offered when you visit someone's home, shops, malls and other public places. Cafe culture is huge in Istanbul and you'll see tons of people sitting in cafes enjoying Turkish çay and kahve over the laughs and conversations. Turkish tea is admired throughout the country and people wouldn't start the day without it whether it's a hot sunny day or a cold day. Turkish tea comes in many flavors but mostly consumed as a black tea with a cube of sugar and lemon when needed. I see people everywhere drinking and enjoying it with many desserts, with and after the meals and in between. It is traditionally served in a teapot and special çay glasses that are a must buy when visiting Türkiye.

Desserts:

If you've got a sweet tooth like me, try traditional Turkish and the modern desserts that are so irresistible, you won't get enough of them. Like the traditional Turkish and modern cuisine varies, Turkish desserts also have a great mix of both! Here are my most recommended desserts to try;

Baklava

One of the best Turkish desserts, Baklava is made from a crispy layer of phyllo dough stuffed with ground pistachios, baked and drenched with sweet honey like syrup. It is one of the most popular desserts in Türkiye and highly recommended.

Künefe/Knafeh

Turkish Künefe is a cheese filled dessert made with kadayif noodles (shredded phyllo), melted cheese, soaked in honey syrup served with ground pistachio on top. I tried Künefe from Hafiz Mustafa on Istiklal street and it is my personal favorite!

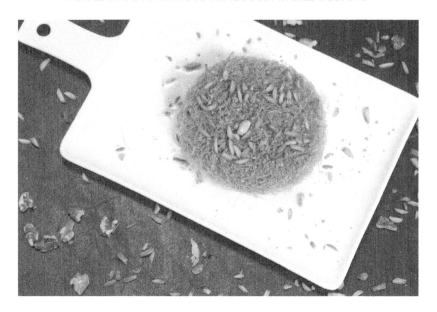

Loküm

Turkish delight or Loküm, is a Turkish delicacy that is a delicate jelly-like dessert based on a mixture of starch and sugar that comes in a variety of colors and flavors. It comes in different shapes like cubes, or cut into slices, or a small bit size piece. Tourists and locals take bundles of gift boxes as a souvenir to give as a gift to their friends and families on special occasions.

Dondurma

Dondurma is the Turkish word for 'Ice Cream'. It is made much like traditional ice cream but two ingredients, mastic and salep are added for stickiness. Famous for its taste and the ice cream tricks on the street where you'll try to catch the cone from the shop vendor but they trick you with 'catch me if you can' and after a few attempts, they'll hand it over to you on a cone. The ice cream is delicious, stretchy and sweet that comes in various flavors.

Strawberry Cake

My Personal favorite dessert on the trip, Strawberry chocolate cake from
Mado restaurant. The picture says it all!

10

How To Avoid Scams and Stay Safe

Istanbul is one of the most visited cities in the world and a safe city for solo male/female travelers, groups or families. Just like any other popular destinations, Istanbul is home to scammers, pocket pickers and opportunists that are waiting to get your phone, cash or other valuable items in crowded touristic areas. But if you are a smart traveler, do your homework and know what kind of scams are common and how to avoid them, you can prepare yourself and make the most out of your trip. Always trust your **instinct**, it is a gift that we all have and can use it to identify the threats. Always be cautious of a situation where things seem 'too good to be true' when shopping for expensive goodsir other similar scenarios. Here are the most common scams that you can avoid and not let the worries ruin your trip.

Taxi Scam

Istanbul has a huge network of Taxis and one of the most common ways of commuting within the city other than the metro. Taxis are relatively cheap but the traffic is terrible in central Istanbul that's why I always prefer to take the Metro, tram or ferry where applicable. If you are a woman and traveling with a child, it's easy and safe to take a private shuttle service which you can book online or ask your hotel to book it for you in advance. If you have to take the taxi, be cautious of few things as below;

Check Driver's License Yellow taxis are cheaper than others, always make sure you are getting in an official taxi that has the 'Taksi' sign and a driver's license displayed on the dashboard.

Check Meter. Make sure they start the meter when the ride begins. Some taxis have the built-in meter in the center mirror and some have the meter installed on the dashboard.

Avoid Long Routes. Clearly show them the hotel or your destination name on google maps or ask them to put it on their GPS and keep your google maps active to track the route if you have the sim card. Some drivers take longer routes to extend the bill. It is usually a 40-50 minutes drive from Istanbul Airport to Taksim or other destinations in Beyoglu district.

Notes/Bills Swap. Make sure to count and check your own notes as they shouldn't be ripped if you are paying by cash. Show the notes and say it loud to the driver before handing over the cash as they can swap big notes with small ones and ask for more money.

Keep Small change. Always keep the change in case you need to pay your fare in 5's, 10's or 20's. They sometimes won't have the change and you'll have to overpay so avoid the situation by keeping small bills with you.

I personally have never experienced any problem in my trips but these are the most common taxi scams to avoid. I'll recommend keeping the contact number of an honest driver if you come across one and travel with him through your trip to avoid using a new taxi every time. You can also use **Bitaksi** or Uber but to my knowledge, the Uber app doesn't work in Istanbul. You may use a VPN to use it and if you happen to find an

Uber, don't pay cash to the driver as it is automatically deducted from your card. I always prefer to commute by Metro, Tram or Ferries as they are the most convenient, affordable and faster way to travel within the center city.

Getting a Drink At a Club and Bar with a friendly 'stranger'

If you are in Taksim or Galata, you might be approached by a friendly local who'll strike up a conversation by giving you a compliment or asking about your travels. He'll invite you to go to a club or a bar where you'll be accompanied by attractive women to get a round of drinks. At the end, you'll be given a huge bill in hundred or thousand of dollars/euros and if you refuse, a bunch of strong and tall men will appear to intimidate you and take you to an ATM machine to make sure you get the funds to pay for the bill. Therefore, always deny on the spot to the 'friendly stranger' to join for a drink at a bar. But if you know any local friends and they take you to a legit club or a bar, then no need to worry and just enjoy the music, let your body move and dance the night away (if you like to dance like me!)

The Currency Conversion Scam

Turkish Lira has seen a drastic decline recently and that makes a great shopping opportunity for tourists. When shopping at local shops, check the currency of the purchase before you swipe your credit card. Some shop traders trick you into paying Euros or Dollars when paying by credit card instead of Turkish lira.

Another conversion scam could be when you are exchanging your Euros or Dollars into local Turkish lira(TRY). Always exchange your currency from a legit exchange where you'll see a lot of other travelers changing their money. You can easily find tons of currency exchange shops that charge minimal or no commission on Taksim Square next to Watsons or on Istiklal Street where you'll see a lot of tourists changing their currencies. Don't exchange your currency from small shops in unknown places or small alleys as some shops may give you counterfeit Turkish liras that will become your liability later on the trip. Scammers who print counterfeit money print big notes like 50 or 100 Liras and that too you can identify by finding the official bank instructions on how to identify the counterfeits. Nevertheless, all legit currency exchanges have machines that count and check the legitimacy of the currency whether its Dollars, Euros or Liras.

Phone and Valuables

It was my second trip to Istanbul and I was strolling in Sultanahmet near Hagia Sophia. I got my phone stolen at the Sultanahmet metro station where I was trying to top up my Istanbulkart at one of the top-up machines. I had my phone in the side pocket of my jacket which had no zip and it was an easy catch from the pickpocketer to slip away my phone. I felt angry, confused and didn't know what to do. I couldn't speak to someone as most people don't speak English. These are common emotions, always try to keep in control, don't panic and take your time to recover your senses. Lesson learnt, i always keep my phone in the front pocket (which i usually do) and luckily, i had an extra phone with me which came in handy. Another tip for all travelers, never put your phone in the back pocket of your jeans which makes it an easy catch for the thieves.

Another incident that happened with an acquaintance as he was wearing a backpack with his passport, cash, cards and valuables and someone cut off the strap of the bag and took everything on Taksim Square. That was a nightmare for him! He had to go to the embassy and get a temporary passport after a long investigation and hassle. On top, he had to borrow funds and his trip was ruined due to carelessness. Always keep your wallet in the front pocket of your pants and wear your backpacks and crossbody bags at the front of your body so you can avoid getting it snatched. This may occur in any crowded tourist areas but can also happen in trams, buses or on a metro. Never leave your belongings unattended when at a cafe, bar or a restaurant, even if it's only for a quick second.

Bottom line, keep your credit cards, passports and cash safe and be careful with your bags, wallets and purses. Always keep them in a safe place and I am repeating, your wallets should never be put in the back pockets. Avoid traveling with a lot of cash or cards in case anything happens. Contact Tourist Police by going to the Tourist Police centers and file a report. It might not get you back your valuables but it is still recommended to do so. The Police report can come-in handy at any given point.

Restaurant Bills for Tourists

If you are a foodie like me and love exploring traditional and contemporary Turkish food, you'll be eating at a lot of places. I didn't have any problem with my bills at any restaurants where I ate but I did hear some tourists complaining online that a few restaurants may add extra items to your bill that you didn't consume. Therefore, be vigilant and check your bill for any extra items before you pay.

11

Tourist Information Centers

Tourist Information centers provide guidance to the tourists about the transportation, sights and the best ways to enjoy your trip. They provide this information through brochures, leaflets, maps etc. Below are the main tourist offices to get your answers on any specific questions;

Sultanahmet Tourism Information Office
Address: Binbirdirek Mah. Divan Yolu Cad. No: 3 At Meydanı Sultanahmet Fatih / Istanbul.
Tel: 0212 518 18 02 / 0212 518 87 54
E-mail: turizmisleri34@ktb.gov.tr
Visiting Hours and Days: Everyday - 09:00 - 17:30

Sirkeci Tourism Information Office
Address: Next to Sirkeci Train Station Ankara Cad. Hocapasa Mah. No: 140 Sirkeci Fatih / Istanbul
Tel: 0212 511 58 88
E-mail: turizmisleri34@ktb.gov.tr
Visiting hours and days: Everyday - 09:00 - 17:30

Taksim Tourism Information Office
Address: Next to AKM, Directorate of State Opera and Ballet entrance floor Taksim / Istanbul
Tel: 0212 233 05 92
E-mail: turizmisleri34@ktb.gov.tr
Visiting hours and days: Every day - 09:00 - 17:30

Sabiha Gökçen Tourism Information Office
Address: International Arrivals Kurtköy / Istanbul
Tel: 0216 588 87 94
E-mail: turizmisleri34@ktb.gov.tr
Visiting hours and days: Everyday - 09:00 - 19:00

Istanbul Airport Tourism Information Office
Address: International Arrivals floor Arnavutköy / Istanbul
Tel: 0212 891 62 05
E-mail: turizmisleri34@ktb.gov.tr
Visiting hours and days: Everyday - 09:00 - 19:00

Galataport Tourism Information office
Address: Kılıçali Paşa Mahallesi, Meclis-i Mebusan Caddesi Beyoglu / Istanbul (Customs area)
E-mail: turizmisleri34@ktb.gov.tr
Visiting hours and days: The hours vary according to the arrival and departure of the ships. Information

Source:
https://istanbul.ktb.gov.tr/EN-284752/tourism-information-offices.html

Emergency Phone Numbers

Police: 155

Ambulance: 112

Fire: 110

Social Support / Women's helpline: 183

Istanbul Tourism Police: +902125274503 mob: +905051876614

email: istanbulturizm@egm.gov.tr

12

Language, Communication Barrier and WiFi

To my surprise, English is not widely spoken through Turkey except those who travel to other English speaking European countries, studied and lived there for a while. When I asked my friend Omar from 'Casa Rosa Suites' in Karaköy, his response was that there's only one English subject taught in the school and the rest of the curriculum is offered in Turkish. I had a hard time speaking to most locals who didn't know basic English either. I found more French and German speakers in Istanbul than English speakers. The best solution is to learn some common Turkish words or use the Google translator as a lot of locals also use translating apps to communicate where needed.

Local Sim and WiFi

If you are trying to get connected to wifi in Istanbul or any other airports in Türkiye, you'll need a European or Turkish number to get the passcode to access the free wifi. Make sure you have your E-visa downloaded prior to departure so you can present it at the airport. Wifi is not very good everywhere in the city and if you are a digital nomad who works and travels, it is important to have a local wifi connection. Restaurants and cafes also have free wifi but it can cause problems for a smooth wifi experience. I always get a local sim from Turkcell, Turk Telecom or Vodafone for a cost of 300 liras more or less, depending on their tourist packages. It includes, local calling, text and upto 10-15 gigs of mobile internet that can last for a good one month or less and you can top up whenever you need it more.

Travel Adapter

It is very important to carry an international adapter that supports the 220 V charging in Turkey. The adapter is **F type** (round shaped with two round pins) which is the basic European outlet. You can also buy it from a local cell phone store that sells phones, sim cards and adapters in Istanbul.

Websites and Apps

Certain websites and apps don't work in Turkey like booking.com and Uber. As advised, you should book your hotels prior to the trip but if you happen to book them on spot, use **otelz.com** which is a local alternative to booking.com. It also gives you free booking, cancellation and good rates. You can always use other websites to book your hotels and accommodations. As for Uber, the app may not work while you are in Istanbul. You may use the VPN or use a local taxi app like **Bitaksi** to get around.

13

Ramadan in Türkiye and Turkish Culture

Ramadan is a holy month where Muslims all over the world fast for thirty days. The fast begins at suhoor - the time of dawn and breaks at Iftar - at the time of sunset. By the end of the month, Ramadan is celebrated with Eid holidays which lasts for 3 days. Traveling to Türkiye in Ramadan can impact your travels. During the day, it is polite to refrain from eating or drinking on the streets as a majority of the Turkish Muslims are fasting but a lot of them also don't fast by choice. Restaurants and cafes are open during the day but not so crowded. Tourists are welcome to eat and drink inside the restaurants. Some bars may not serve alcoholic beverages during the holy month.

At sunset, Istanbul starts to get back into full swing. Streets, restaurants and cafes get crowded for the iftar (breaking the fast). Streets, stores and mosques are decorated, festival lights, special signs are displayed and it feels like a carnival in the city. Most of the restaurants get packed for the iftar dinner offering a special menu and it's hard to get a table unless you make a reservation. Malls and shops are open during the day and night and offer special promotions. One aspect of Ramadan that may bother you is the drummers going around the streets mostly away from tourist areas, beating their drums to wake up the locals for the suhoor, before the time of Dawn.

Rest assured, traveling to Istanbul in Ramadan is one of a kind experience and is different from the rest of the year. Hospitality is at its peak and so are the festivities during the holy month. Below are the dates for Ramadan in 2022 and 2023 year;

- **2022. Saturday, April 02 – Monday, May 02**
- **2023. Wednesday, Mar 23 – Thursday, Apr 20**

Turkish Culture

Türkiye has centuries old rich history and culture evolved from Byzantine and Ottoman empires. For decades, people have been visiting Türkiye and enjoying the unique traditions, customs, historical sights, most delicious food and a variety of the landscape. Turkish people are friendly, helpful, respectful and love to host tourists. Especially in rural areas, the host will love to share their slice of bread, food and drinks to friends, neighbors and strangers. The culture of families is very strong and considered most important. Youngsters give a lot of respect to the elderly people. Relations with neighbors are close and friendships are strong among local communities.

Interestingly, a very popular symbol of blue beaded decor and accessories called 'nazar boncugu' is seen all across the country in homes, restaurants, cafes, offices and cars. The trend has become global and is used in textiles, earring, necklaces, bracelets, wind chimes, rugs, shirts and all sorts of items. Definitely a buy recommendation as one of the symbolic Turkish souvenirs. It's easy to connect with people and the culture even if you don't know the language. Relax, breathe and enjoy the culture and hospitality of Turkish people.

Public Holidays 2022

Travelers who want to travel and plan it in-advance, should look into the holiday calendar and plan accordingly. Other than Ramadan Feast and Sacrifice Feast holidays which are mostly celebrated for three to four days, no other holidays would significantly impact your traveling.

01 Jan. New Year's Day

    20 Mar. March Equinox

    23 Apr. National Sovereignty and Children's Day

    1 May. Labor and Solidarity Day

1 May. Ramadan Feast Eve

2 - 4 May. Eid ul Fitr Holidays / Ramadan Feast Holidays

19 May. Commemoration of Atatuürk, Youth and Sports Day

21 Jun. June Solstice

8 Jul. Sacrifice Feast Eve

9 - 12 Jul. Eid ul Adha Holidays / Sacrifice Feast Holidays

15 Jul. Democracy and National Unity Day

30 Aug. Victory Day

23 Sep. September Equinox

28 Oct. Republic Day Eve

29 Oct. Republic Day

10 Nov. Ataturk Memorial Day

22 Dec. December Solstice

31 Dec. New Year's Eve

Source: www.timeanddate.com

14

Conclusion

As I intended before writing, my goal is to give my fellow travelers and readers a compact travel guide full of knowledge, tips and suggestions on how to plan well and make the most out of their trip. I hope you like all of my top recommendations for what to do, see and taste and how to stay safe during your stay in Istanbul. I have put in all the necessary information that is current and will help anyone traveling to Istanbul in 2022 and beyond. I really hope you enjoy the book as much as I have enjoyed writing it! And that it has helped make your trip to Istanbul more fun and memorable. Enjoy your stay in Istanbul!

If you found this book helpful, I'd be very appreciative if you left a favorable review for the book on Amazon.

15

Resources

YEŞ, Y. (2021, April 15). *Istanbul Skyline During the Sunset*. Pexels. Retrieved July 21, 2022, from https://www.pexels.com/photo/istanbul-skyline-during-the-sunset-7524199/

worldweatheronline.com. (n.d.). *Istanbul climate weather averages*. World Weather Online. Retrieved July 21, 2022, from https://www.worldweatheronline.com/istanbul-weather-averages/istanbul/tr.aspx

Contributors to Wikimedia projects. (n.d.). *New Istanbul airport route*. WikiVoyage. Retrieved July 22, 2022, from https://en.wikivoyage.org/wiki/Istanbul

Wikitravel.org. (n.d.). *Sabiha Gökçen international airport*. Wikitravel. Retrieved July 21, 2022, from https://en.wikivoyage.org/wiki/Istanbul

Khalil, A. (2021a, April 17). *City square with people and buildings near vehicles*. Pexels. Retrieved July 21, 2022, from https://www.pexels.com/photo/city-square-with-people-and-buildings-near-vehicles-7542167/

Hovee, N. (2020, October 6). *İstanbul, İstanbul, Turkey*. Pexels. Retrieved July 21, 2022, from https://www.pexels.com/photo/suleymaniye-mosque-under-evening-sky-5063804/

Teke, S. (2020, February 11). *İstanbul, Turkey*. Pexels. Retrieved July 21, 2022, from https://www.pexels.com/photo/brown-concrete-buildin g-under-blue-sky-3684396/

Khalil, A. (2021, April 17). *Ship floating in city on cloudy day*. Pexels. Retrieved July 21, 2022, from https://www.pexels.com/photo/ship-floating-in-city-in-cloudy-day-7542145/

Татьяна. (2021, August 16). *Restaurant on the street*. Pexels. Retrieved July 21, 2022, from https://www.pexels.com/photo/restaurant-on-the-street-9330580/

Khalil, A. (2021a, April 17). *Ornamental ceiling with arched windows in market*. Pexels. Retrieved July 21, 2022, from https://www.pexels.com /photo/ornamental-ceiling-with-arched-windows-in-market-7542 101/

Taner, E. (2020, October 19). *Taksim, people walking*. Unsplash. Retrieved July 21, 2022, from https://unsplash.com/photos/sH2f0 qBgDUA

Dolovac, H. (n.d.). *Archeological Museum*. Pexels. Retrieved July 21, 2022, from https://www.pexels.com/photo/people-in-front-o-the-archaeological-museum-in-istanbul-7918228/

Dana @Elmanana. (2021, August 9). *Breathtaking Byzantine mosaics of the 14th century at the Chora Church, Istanbul*. Unsplash. Retrieved July 21, 2022, from https://unsplash.com/photos/PZ7aUU89wSI

Kahveci, M. K. (2021, May 24). *The Staircase of the Dolmabahçe Palace*. Pexels. Retrieved July 21, 2022, from https://www.pexels.com/photo/ the-staircase-of-the-dolmabahce-palace-8011546/

Aksu, S. (2021, December 12). *Beautiful concrete entrance door*. Pexels.

Retrieved July 21, 2022, from https://www.pexels.com/photo/beautif
ul-concrete-entrance-door-10529467/

GÜMÜŞSOY, A. L. P. E. R. E. N. (2021, March 2). *The Topkapi palace in Istanbul*. Pexels. Retrieved July 21, 2022, from https://www.pexels.co
m/photo/the-topkapi-palace-in-istanbul-7000995/

Akyurt, E. (2020, October 7). *People shopping at spice bazaar in istanbul*. Pexels. Retrieved July 21, 2022, from https://www.pexels.com/photo/
people-shopping-at-spice-spice-bazaar-in-istanbul-5096971/

Pan, W. (2016, August 24). *Lanterns at a bazaar*. Unsplash. Retrieved July 21, 2022, fromhttps://unsplash.com/photos/eBE3pEIZjbcutm_
source=unsplash&utm_medium=referral&utm_content=creditShar
eLink

Colman, D. (2021, March 21). *The blue mosque in Istanbul*. Pexels. Retrieved July 21, 2022, from https://www.pexels.com/photo/the-blu
e-mosque-in-istanbul-7198471/

Volk, J. (2020, December 20). *Main dome with colourful ornamental elements in blue mosque*. Pexels. Retrieved July 21, 2022, from https://w
ww.pexels.com/photo/main-dome-with-colorful-ornamental-ele
ments-in-blue-mosque-6118471/

C. (2020, September 30). *Republic monument at taksim square*. Pexels. Retrieved July 21, 2022, from https://www.pexels.com/photo/the-rep
ublic-monument-at-taksim-square-4897162/

Tarampi, R. (2017, March 21). *Trolley in the snow*. Unsplash. Retrieved July 21, 2022, fromhttps://unsplash.com/photos/a5KMylND9Bo?utm

_source=unsplash&utm_medium=referral&utm_content=creditSh
areLink

Çetin, S. (2019, March 17). *Low-angle Photograph of Concrete Tower*. Pexels. https://www.pexels.com/photo/low-angle-photograph-of-concrete-tower-2042109/

Shamsul, A. (2018, February 18). *Brown-bigbus-istanbul-traveling-on-road-near-brown-dome-building*. Pexels. Retrieved July 21, 2022, from https://www.pexels.com/photo/brown-bigbus-istanbul-traveling-on-road-near-brown-dome-building-879478/

SOLOMONIK, V. (2021, June 10). *Turkish coffee is made on the sand in the streets of Istanbul*. Unsplash. Retrieved July 21, 2022, from https://unsplash.com/photos/xdX-qxudOTM?utm_source=unsplash&utm_medium=referral&utm_content=creditShareLink

Svklimkin @Svklimkin.Com, S. (2019, August 20). *Dancing dervishes. Istanbul*. Unsplash. Retrieved July 21, 2022, from https://unsplash.com/photos/inJoURyO-Ww?utm_source=unsplash&utm_medium=referral&utm_content=creditShareLink

Polat, A. (2021, September 2). *View of the Suleymaniye Mosque*. Pexels. Retrieved July 21, 2022, from https://www.pexels.com/photo/view-of-the-suleymaniye-mosque-9415461/

Ahmetler, T. (2022, February 21). *Yellow Motor Scooter Parked Beside a Store*. Pexels. Retrieved July 21, 2022, from https://www.pexels.com/photo/yellow-motor-scooter-parked-beside-a-store-11253644/

Arman, E. (2021, May 28). *Man Sitting on Pier Looking at White Boat on Water During Sunset in Istanbul.* Pexels. Retrieved July 21, 2022, from https://www.pexels.com/photo/man-sitting-on-pier-looking -at-white-boat-on-water-during-sunset-in-istanbul-8105547/

Orlova, M. (2020, July 24). *Ornamental arched ceiling in hammam.* Pexels. Retrieved July 21, 2022, from https://www.pexels.com/photo/ ornamental-arched-ceiling-in-hammam-4946756/

Gonullu, M. (2021, March 24). *Sliced-bread-on-brown-wooden- chopping-board.* Pexels. Retrieved July 21, 2022, from https://ww w.pexels.com/photo/sliced-bread-on-brown-wooden-chopping- board-7243335/

COŞKUN, A. Y. L. A. (2021, August 8). *A look at börek, with 3 recipes to try at home.* Dailysabah. Retrieved July 21, 2022, from https://www.dai lysabah.com/life/food/a-look-at-borek-with-3-recipes-to-try-at- home

Mukkath, S. (2020, October 24). *Turkish-pide-flat-bread-with-ground- meat.* Pexels. Retrieved July 21, 2022, from https://www.pexels.com/ photo/turkish-pide-flat-bread-with-ground-meat-5639357/

Iskender Kebab House. (n.d.). *Iskender Kebab – Istanbul Kebab House.* Istanbulhouse.Ca. Retrieved July 21, 2022, from https://istanbulhous e.ca/foodmenu/iskender-kebab/

Daboul, S. (2019, May 4). *Grilled meat on skewers.* Pexels. Retrieved July 21, 2022, from https://www.pexels.com/photo/grilled-meats-o n-skewers-2233729/

Fitria, F. (2021, April 20). *Lahmacun.* Pexels. Retrieved July 21, 2022, from https://www.pexels.com/photo/bread-food-pizza-restaurant-7545570/

AYTAR, S. A. Y. G. I. N. (2021, November 13). *Kumpir*. Unsplash. Retrieved July 21, 2022, fromhttps://unsplash.com/photos/2giRffIqn Ckutm_source=unsplash&utm_medium=referral&utm_content=cr editShareLink

Ibrahimzade, F. (2020, September 11). *Beef meat burger with tomato sauce*. Unsplash. Retrieved July 21, 2022, from https://unsplash.com/ photos/IonMINY06XE?utm_source=unsplash&utm_medium=refer ral&utm_content=creditShareLink

Tumer, F. (2021, August 4). *Flat Lay Photography of Adana Kebab on Wooden Plate*. Pexels. Retrieved July 21, 2022, from https://www.pexe ls.com/photo/flat-lay-photography-of-adana-kebab-on-wooden-plate-7439809/

Mallah, A. A. (2022, January 10). *Turkish Coffee on a Brass Cup*. Pexels. Retrieved July 21, 2022, from https://www.pexels.com/photo/turkish-coffee-on-a-brass-cup-10809641/

Lisa, L. (2021, April 4). *Close-Up Shot of a Glass of Tea on a Saucer*. Pexels. Retrieved July 21, 2022, from https://www.pexels.com/photo/close-up-shot-of-a-glass-of-tea-on-a-saucer-7393906/

Akyurt, E. (2021, May 6). *Baklava on Box*. Pexels. Retrieved July 21, 2022, from https://www.pexels.com/photo/baklava-on-box-780311 7/

Mukkath, S. (2020, December 23). *Overhead Shot of Knafeh*. Pexels.

Retrieved July 21, 2022, from https://www.pexels.com/photo/overhe ad-shot-of-knafeh-6271902/

Gonullu, M. (2020, December 11). *Assortment of sugar starch cubes sprinkled with powdered sugar.* Pexels. Retrieved July 21, 2022, from https://www.pexels.com/photo/assortment-of-sugar-starch-cubes -sprinkled-with-powdered-sugar-6161509/

Ahmed, A. (2021, June 5). *A Man in Turkish Traditional Clothing Serving a Customer.* Pexels. Retrieved July 21, 2022, from https://www.pex els.com/photo/a-man-in-turkish-traditional-clothing-serving-a-customer-8218836/

istanbul.ktb.gov.tr. (n.d.). *Tourism Information Offices.* Retrieved July 21, 2022, from https://istanbul.ktb.gov.tr/EN-284752/tourism-infor mation-offices.html

Akyurt, E. (2022, May 16). *Evil eye beads hanging on the wall.* Pexels. Retrieved July 21, 2022, from https://www.pexels.com/photo/evil-ey e-beads-hanging-on-the-wall-12133987/

timeanddate.com. (n.d.). *Year 2022 Calendar - Turkey.* Retrieved July 21, 2022, from https://www.timeanddate.com/calendar/custom.html ?country=4&year=2022&hol=281

Göncü, T. C. (2019). *DOLMABAHÇE PALACE AS THE ADMINISTRATIVE CENTER AND EMBLEM OF THE TANZIMAT.* Https://Istanbultarihi.Ist/. Retrieved July 21, 2022, from https://istanbultarihi.ist/449-dolma bahce-palace-as-the-administrative-center-and-emblem-of-the-tanzimat